Why Do I Sing?

Animal Songs of the Pacific Northwest

Jennifer Blomgren

Illustrated by Andrea Gabriel

SASQUATCH BOOKS
SEATTLE

Why do I sing in the brightness of day,
On a fence near a sweet-smelling field of mown hay,
While overhead arches a sky of bright blue?

I'm a MEADOWLARK singing for you.

The SPOTTED OWL sings a song in the night
That rings through the air lit by stars soft and bright.
He calls to the treetops and new moon above.
Maybe he's singing for love.

Gathered 'round a golden campfire, why do we sing?

In the cool, still evening air, our clear, high voices ring.

Everybody sings; every girl, every boy.

For the best of all reasons: We sing for joy.

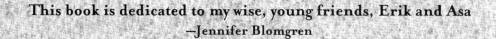

This book is dedicated to my wise, young friends, Erik and Asa
—Jennifer Blomgren

Dedicated with love to Sara and Sydney Hardwick, who are a constant source of joy and inspiration
—Andrea Gabriel

Manufactured in China by C&C Offset Printing Co. Ltd. Shanghai, in June 2013

Published by Sasquatch Books
17 16 15 14 13   9 8 7 6 5 4 3 2 1

Editor: Gary Luke
Project editor: Michelle Hope Anderson
Illustrations: Andrea Gabriel
Design and composition: Sarah Plein

Library of Congress Cataloging-in-Publication Data is available.

ISBN: 978-1-57061-845-1

Sasquatch Books
1904 Third Avenue, Suite 710
Seattle, WA 98101
(206) 467-4300
www.sasquatchbooks.com
custserv@sasquatchbooks.com